Let's Find Out About Names

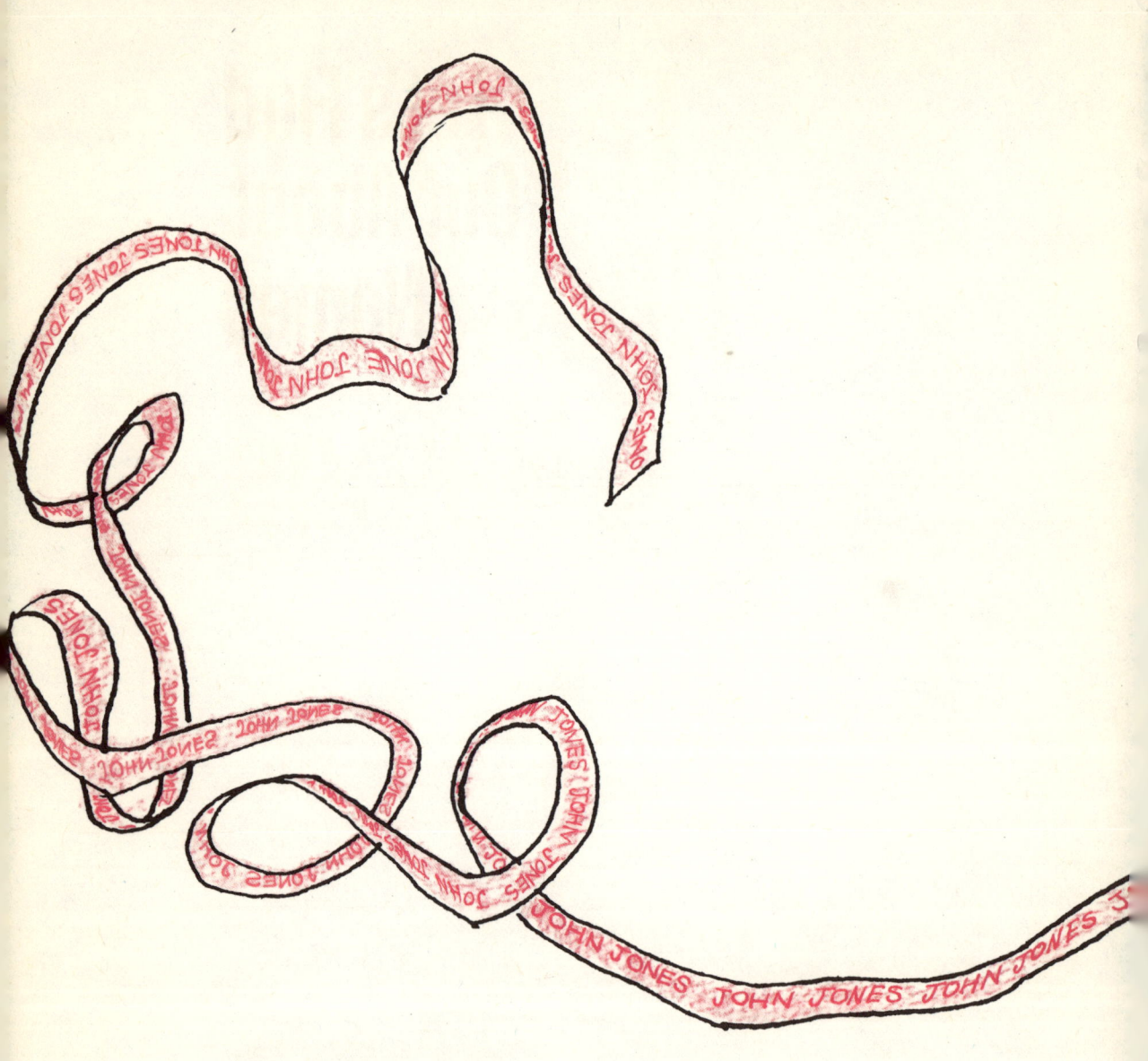

Franklin Watts, Inc.
845 Third Avenue, New York, N.Y. 10022

Let's Find Out About Names

by Valerie Pitt
pictures by Pat Grant Porter

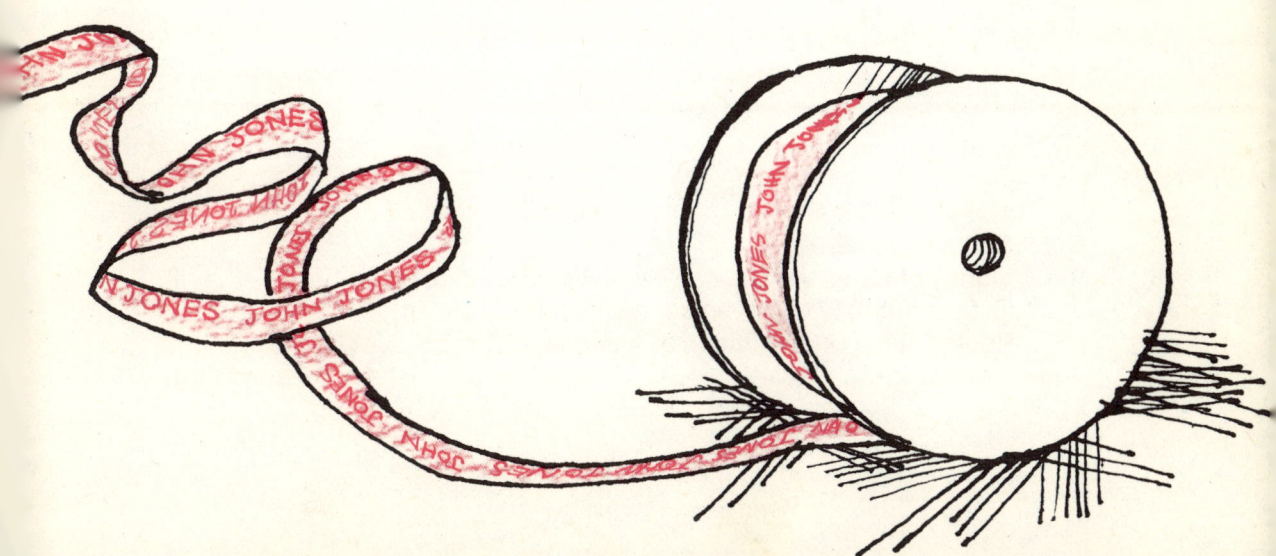

10 9 8 7 6 5 4 3
SBN 531-00069-9
Library of Congress Catalog Card Number: 76-131156
© Copyright 1971 by Franklin Watts, Inc.
Printed in the United States of America

Let's Find Out About Names

Can you imagine what the world would be like if there were no such things as names?
We might be called by numbers instead.
It is doubtful you would be called a simple 9 or 11, because there are millions of people in the world who would have to come before you.
You might be number 3,470,102,397.

Think of the confusion when you made a telephone call and the operator asked, "Who is calling, please?"
Or think how long it would take your teacher to read the class roll call.

No, thank goodness we have names.
Names are a personal, easy way of telling
   who people are.
Your name is part of you and no one else.
It is your own private property.

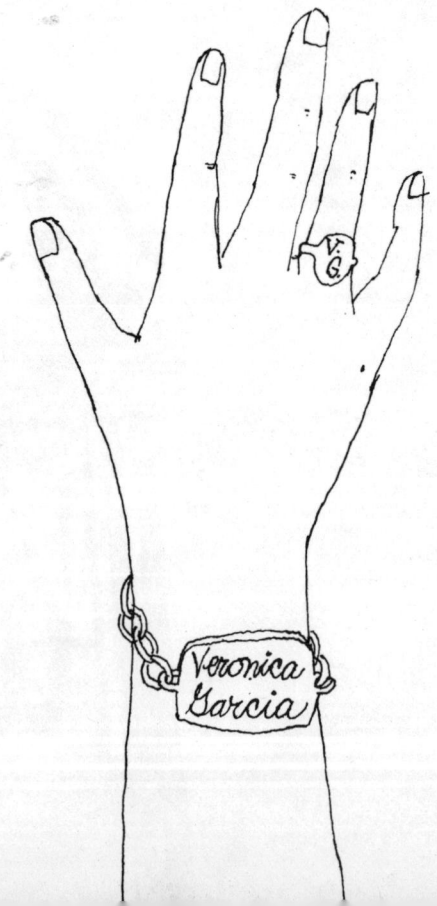

Everyone has at least two names—
   his first name and his last name.
Everyone has at least two initials, also.
First names are called Christian names.
Last names are called surnames.
Which is the surname in this name—William
   Patrick Fowler?

Some people have a middle name, too.
William Fowler's middle name is Patrick.
Some people have two, three, or four middle names.
Prince Charles of England has three middle names.
His full name is Charles Philip Arthur George, Prince of Wales.

Surnames, or last names, are family names. When a woman marries, she usually drops her last name and takes on her husband's surname.

Children take the surname of their father, too.
So everyone in the family has the same name.
You might be part of the Rublowsky family, or the Rosenbaum family, or the Smith family.

Long ago, people did not have surnames.
They were known just by their Christian names.
But as more and more people were born, things got very confusing.
When someone called Alan's name, did he mean Alan the father or Alan the son?
So in time, Alan's son took on the last name of Alanson.
The name Alanson separated the son from the father, but showed they were part of the same family.

In the same way, the son of John became Johnson.
How many more last names can you think of, ending in -son?
There are Robinson, Williamson...

Many last names have been handed down for hundreds of years.

The first people named Wood may once have lived beside a wood or may have been woodcutters.

The first person called Shepard may have been a shepherd in the fields.

The first person named Taylor was probably a tailor, sewing and cutting cloth for his neighbors.

These names are "occupational" names because they described what a man did for a living—what his occupation was.

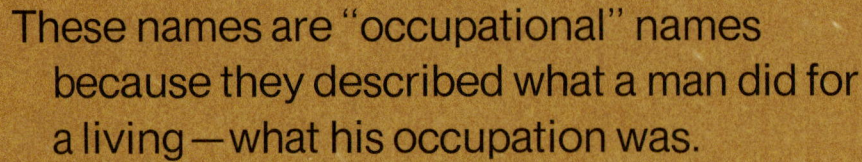

There are lots of other occupational names still in use, though they may not describe the man's job today.
Can you think of any?
There are Baker, Farmer, Smith…

Some last names are descriptive names. Perhaps the first person with the surname of Hardy was a strong man who could hunt and fish for hours without tiring.

There are other descriptive names, too, like Short and Longfellow.

Because people have to have definite ways of telling one person from another, we have Christian names as well as surnames.
Your parents chose your first name because they liked it and thought it was a good name for you.

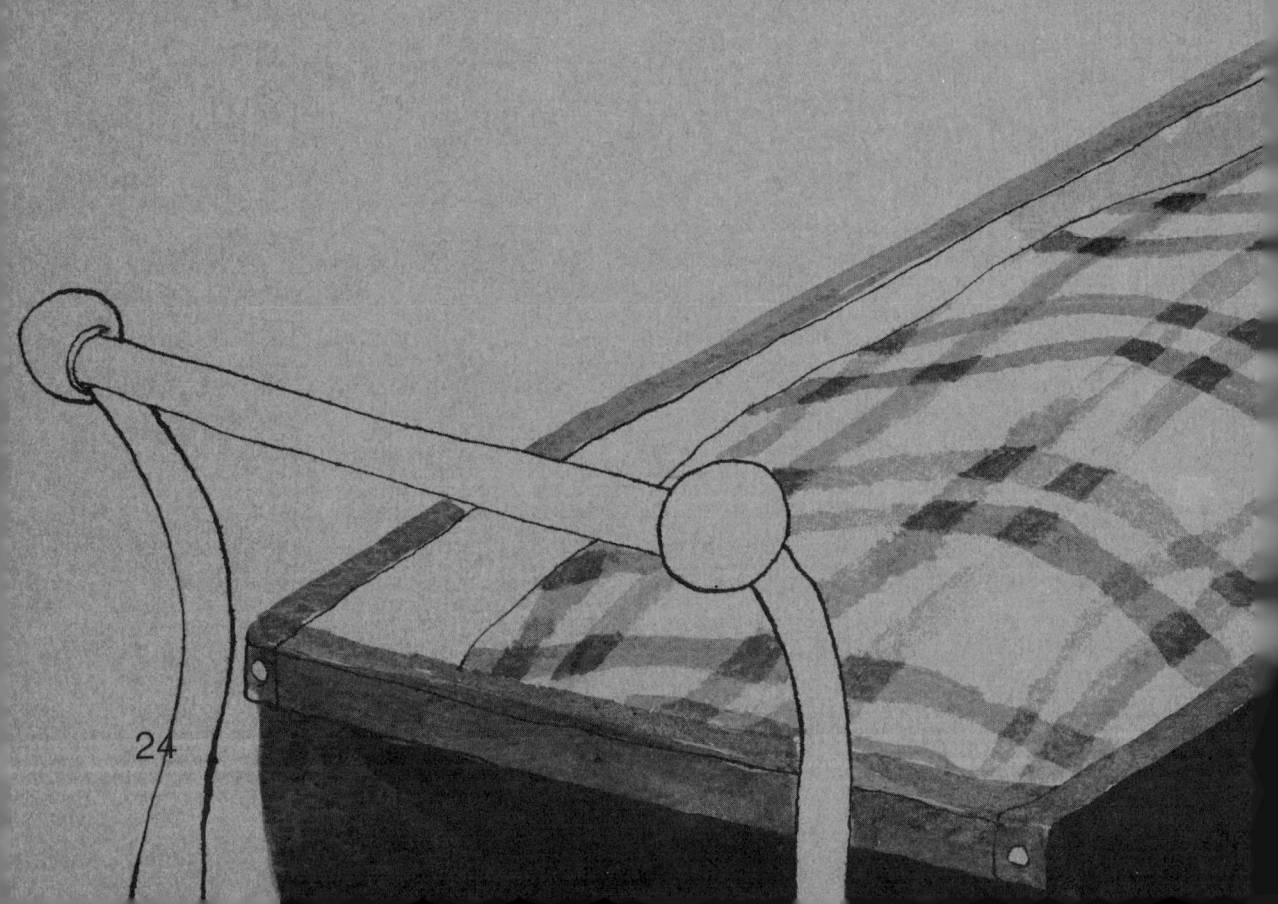

Some families hand down the same name again and again.
If both you and your father are called James, you will add Junior to your name.

If your grandfather is living and is also called James, you will be James III — the third James.

Do you know why your parents chose your name?
Perhaps it was a family favorite, or maybe you were named after a poem, or a song, or a book, or a flower, or perhaps a nice aunt.

Most names have definite meanings.
The name John is from the Hebrew, and means "God is gracious."
There are lots of "John"'s around the world in many different languages.
In France they are Jean—in Spain, Juan—in Germany, Johannes—in Holland, Jan—in Italy, Giovanni—in Russia, Ivan.

The feminine forms of John are Jane and Jean. These names are loved around the world. The French say Jeanne—the Germans, Johanna—the Italians, Giovanna—the Spanish, Juana.

Most of the countries of the world are linked together by names.

Do you know a Vanessa?
Vanessa means "butterfly."
Irene means "peace."
Clara means "bright" or "clear."
Eve means "life."
Catherine means "pure."
Ann means "grace."
Patricia means "noble."

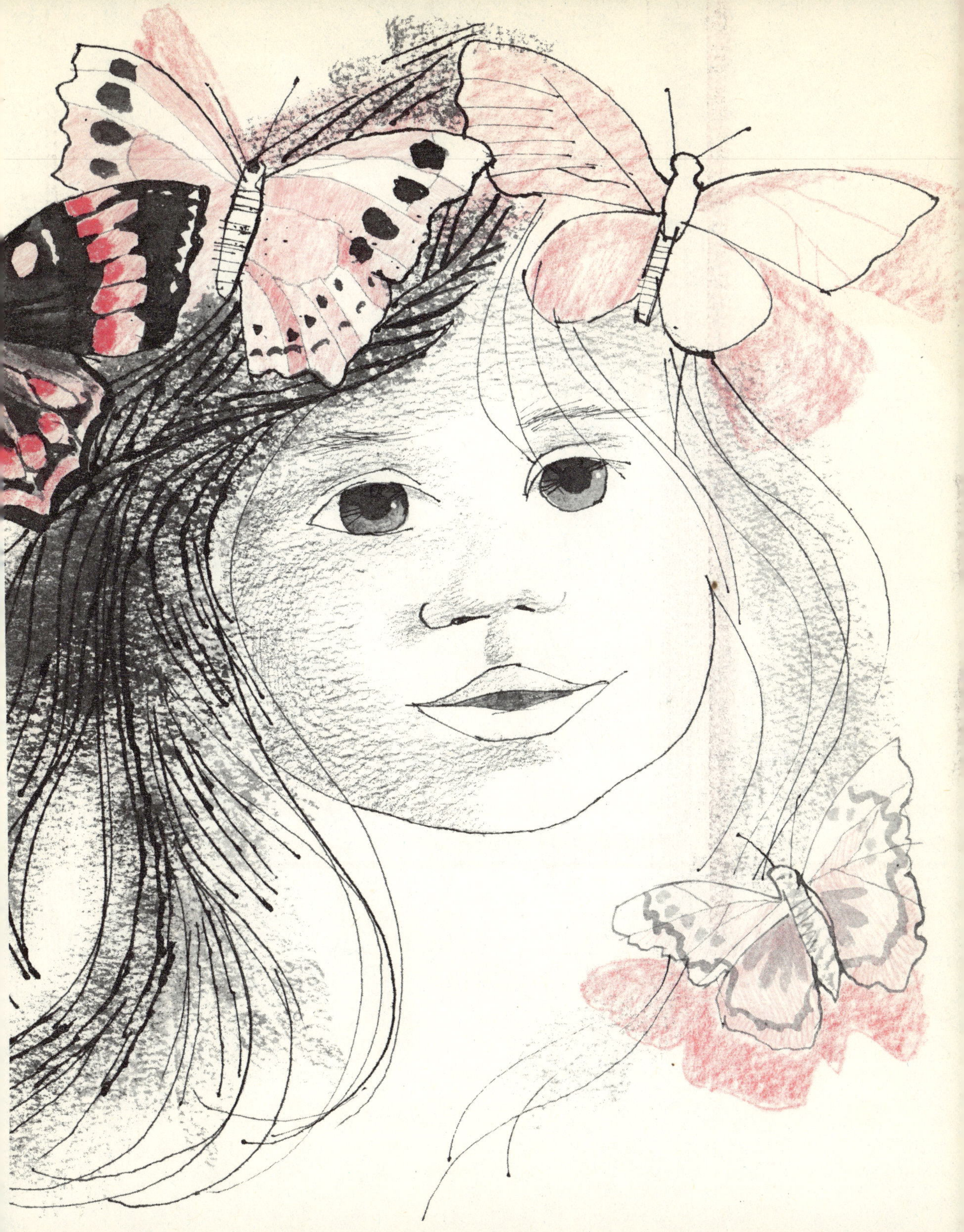

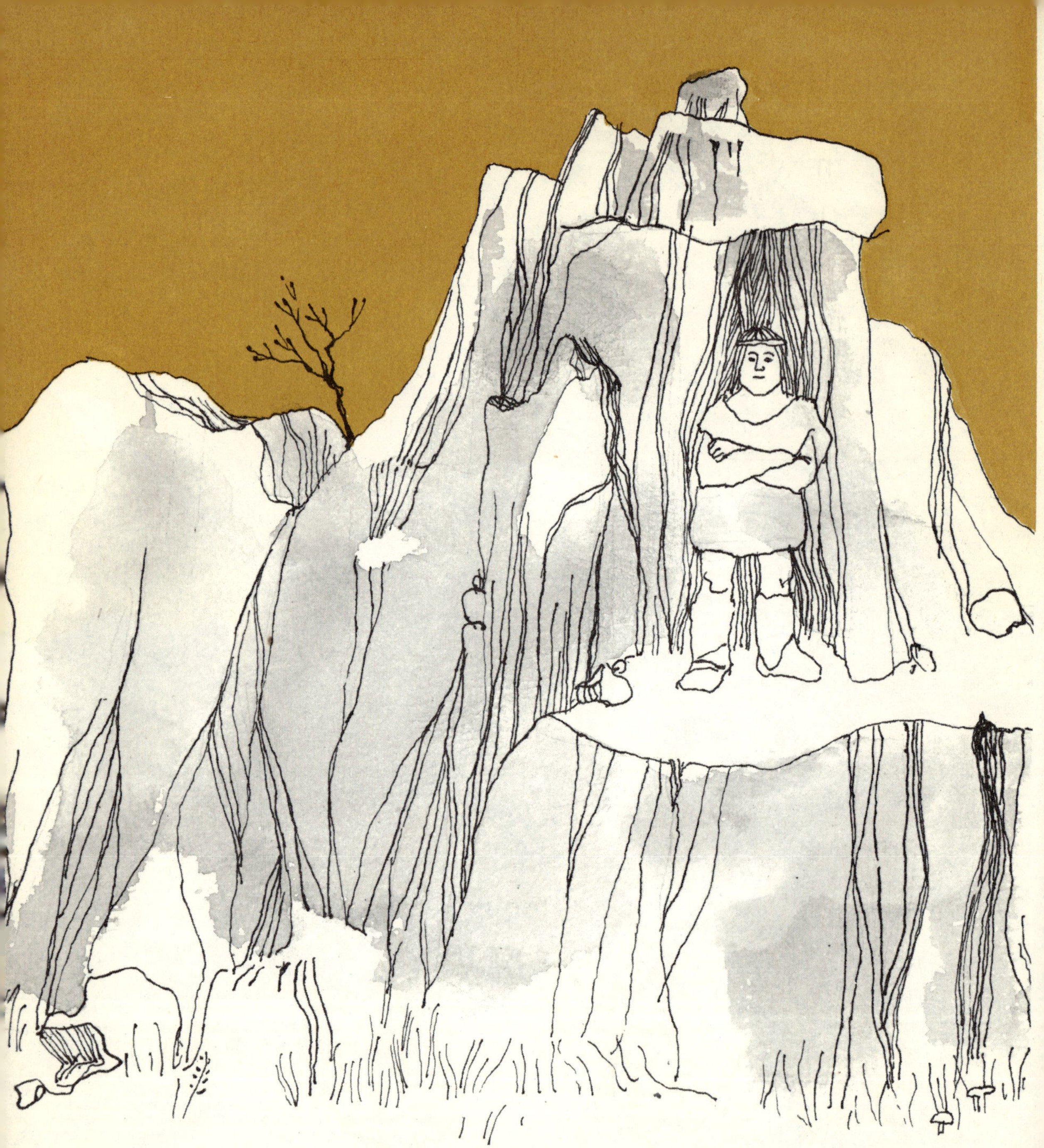

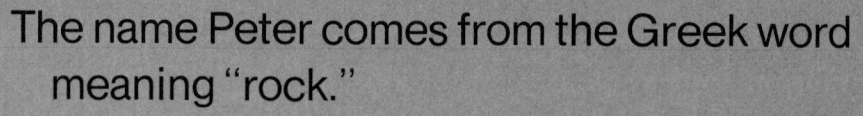

The name Peter comes from the Greek word meaning "rock."
Perhaps it was first given to a strong, firm person.
William means "strong protector."

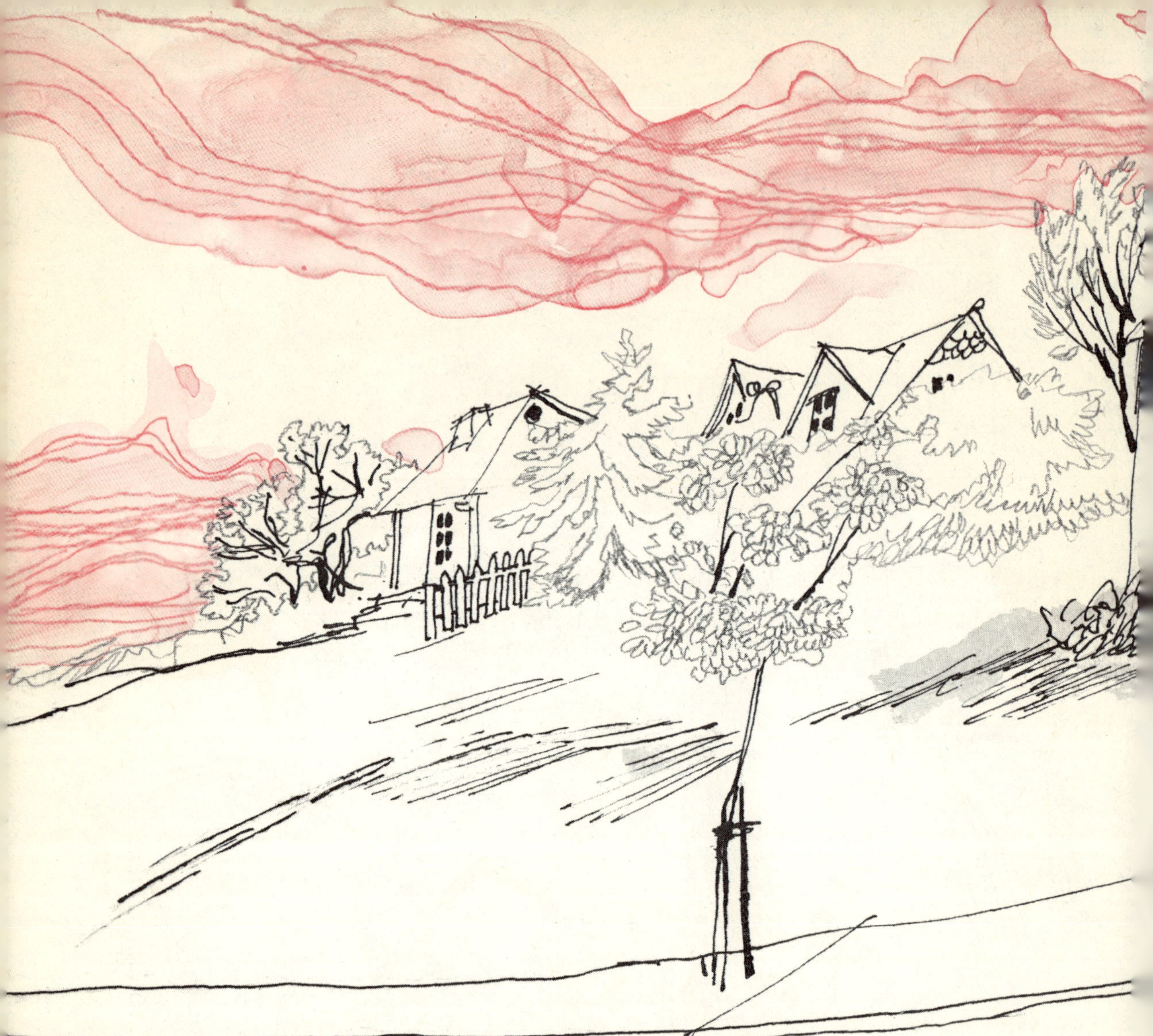

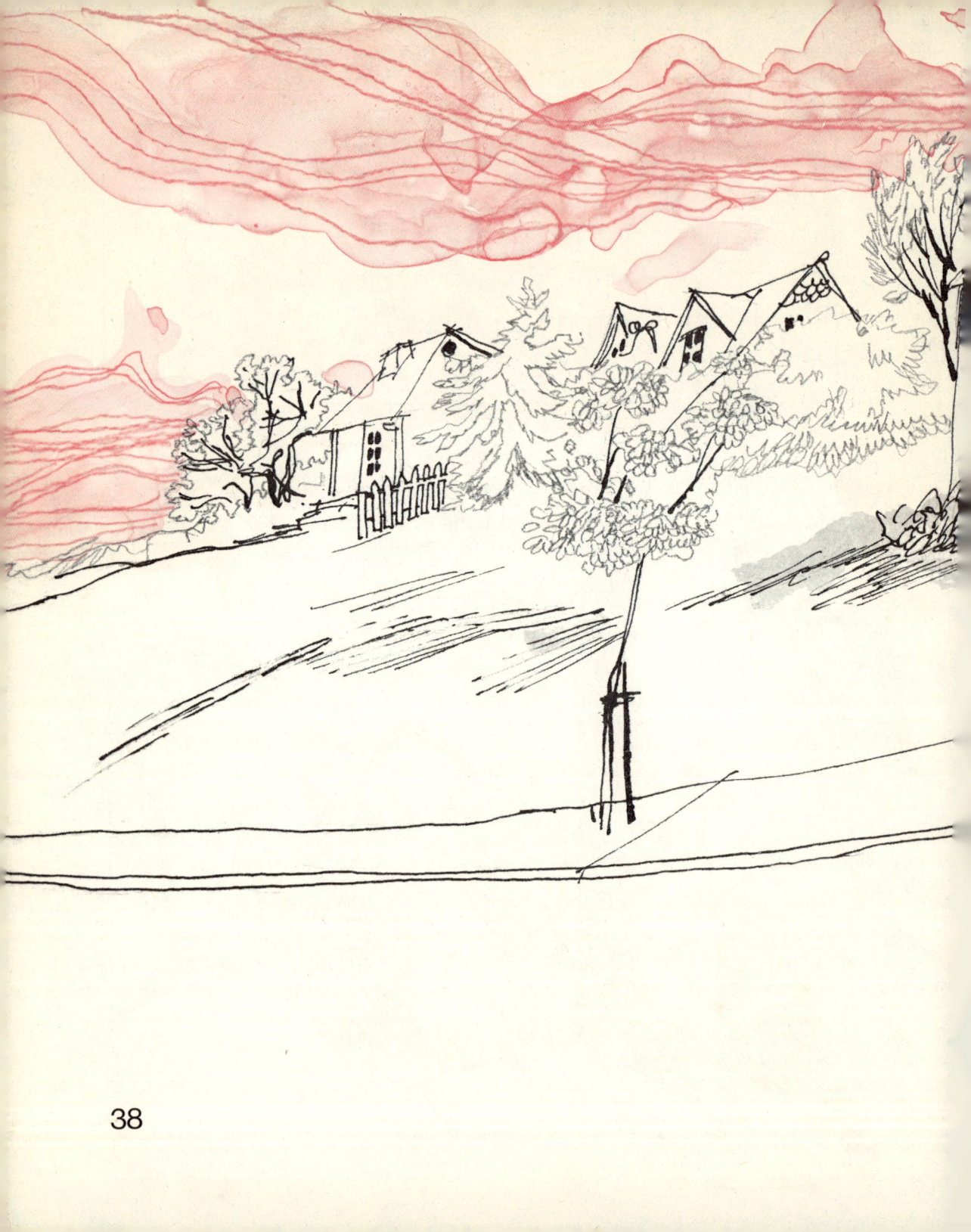

What is *your* name?
If you want to find out what your name means, go to the library and ask for a book on the meaning of names.
You will probably find your name there.

Because your name is yours alone, it comes to mean many things to people who know you.

It means things like—who you are, what you look like, what you are like.

That is why if we like someone, their name takes on special meaning.

It stands for the good feelings we have about that person.

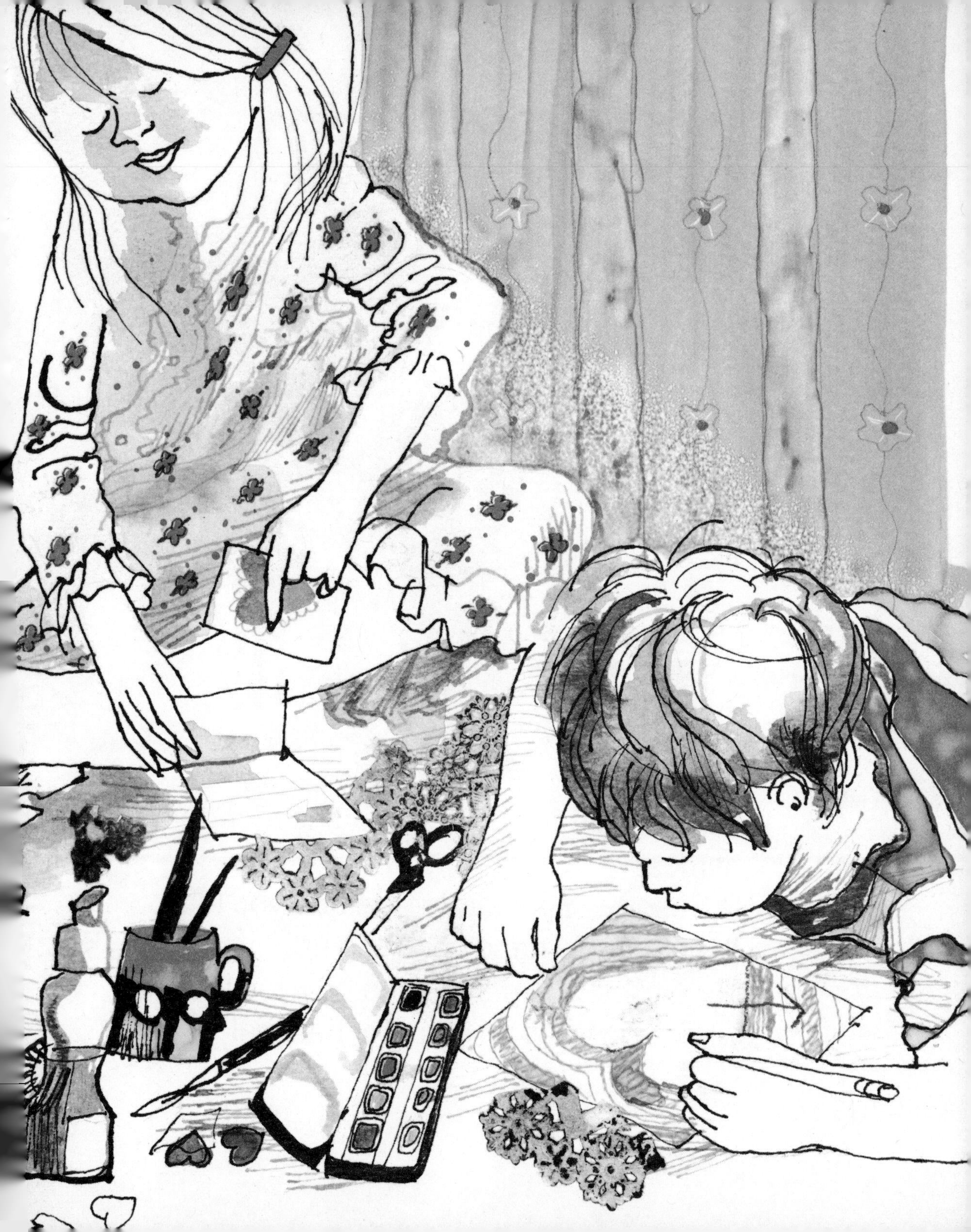

What do you think of when you hear certain names?

Ella Sandow. She may be the one you look for when you need cheering up.

Jerry Angelo. He may be the boy you look for when you need an extra for baseball.

Andrew Blum. He may be your friend who loves to read and experiment with his chemistry set.
Perhaps you call him Professor or Prof. "Professor" is his nickname.

44

Some people are known by their nicknames
 more often than by their regular names.
Some nicknames are just cruel and silly,
 but others may tell more about a person
 than his real name does.
Do you have a nickname?

Sometimes friends who want to have a special name for you shorten or change your real name.
A poet wrote a rhyme about it:
"Father calls me William,
Sister calls me Will,
Mother calls me Willie,
But the fellows call me Bill."

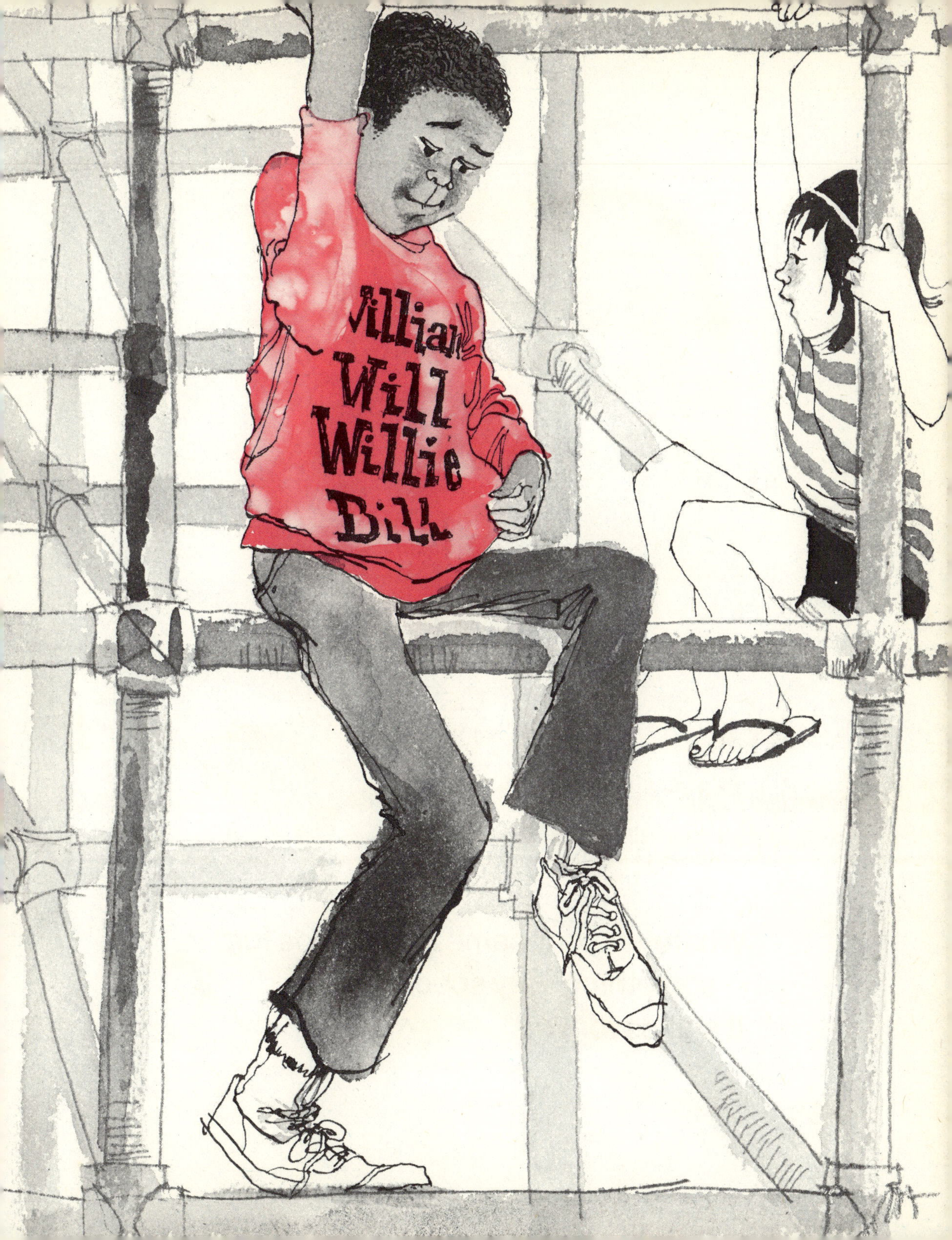
William
Will
Willie
Bill

Whatever your name is, it stands for something very special.
It stands for *you*.

BANGOR ELEMENTARY LIBRARY